WHAT *IS* IT THAT MAKES US WHAT WE *ARE*?

WHAT IS IT THAT *DEFINES* US? IS IT WHERE WE *LIVE*? IS IT OUR *SCHOOLING*?

OR IS IT OUR *FAMILY*?

ALEX RIDER.

FAMILY. HAVE YOU *PREPARED* SOMETHING FOR US?

OH! UM... YES.

COME ON, THEN.

GO ON.

YEAH.

OK.

"YOU KNOW..."

PORT TALLON
Welcomes
Careful Drivers

"...LIFE IN THE **SLOW LANE.**"

KER

'DUNK!

"THE THING ABOUT MY UNCLE IS, HE'S NOT VERY EASY TO *PIN DOWN*."

BRAKKA BRAKKA BRAKKA B

?

SCREEEEECH

!?

VRRRRRM

RI D3R

"I WOULDN'T SAY *I* WAS MUCH LIKE HIM..."

BEETHOVEN
DISC 3 02:56

BEEP

WHIRRRR

KLIK!

FRONT MISSILE LAUNCH
REAR MISSILE LAUNCH
EJECTOR SEAT

FRONT MIS

TARGET LOCKED

REA MISS

DIT

DIT

DIIIIIIII...

"...AND I DON'T THINK ANYONE **MAKES** US WHAT WE ARE."

"I THINK WE JUST **ARE**."

THE NEW STORMBREAKER
YOUR SCHOOL WILL HAVE ONE SOON

THAT WAS **REALLY SAD** ABOUT HAVING NO MUM AND DAD, ALEX.

YOU'RE SUCH A **LOSER**!

WHY DON'T YOU JUST **GET LOST**, GARY?

BULLIES ARE SO... **LAST YEAR**.

HEY, SABINA.

OH...

HI, ALEX.

I WAS **WONDERING**... DO YOU WANT TO **DO** SOMETHING THIS WEEKEND?

NO.

I MEAN, **I CAN'T**.

I HAVE **RIDING LESSONS** ON SATURDAY, AND THEN I'M GOING **OUT** WITH MY MUM AND DAD.

OH!

SORRY...

IT DOESN'T MATTER.

MAYBE **NEXT** WEEKEND!

WHATEVER.

BEEP BEEP

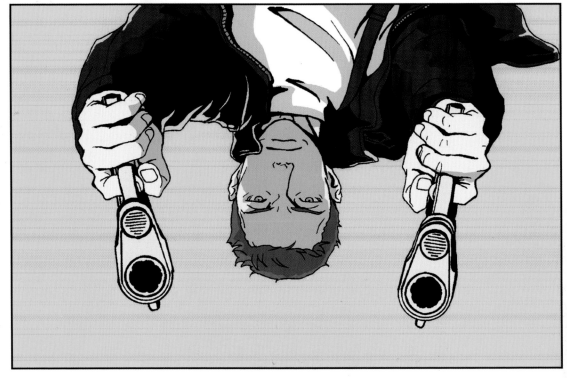

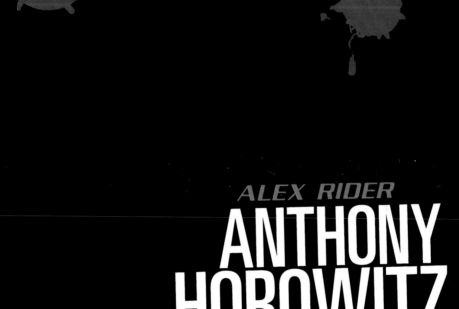

ALEX RIDER

ANTHONY HOROWITZ

ANTONY JOHNSTON
KANAKO AND YUZURU

THE GRAPHIC NOVEL
WALKER

STORMBREAKER

First published 2006 by Walker Books Ltd
87 Vauxhall Walk, London SE I I 5HJ

This edition published 2012

2 4 6 8 10 9 7 5 3

Text and illustrations © 2006 Walker Books Ltd
Based on the original novel Stormbreaker © 2000 Stormbreaker Productions Ltd
Screenplay © MMVI Samuelsons / IoM Film
Film © MMVI Film and Entertainment
VIP Medienfonds 4 GmbH & Co. KG and UK Film Council
Style Guide © MMVI ARR Ltd

Anthony Horowitz has asserted his moral rights.

Trademarks © 2006 Stormbreaker Productions Ltd
Stormbreaker™, Alex Rider™, Boy with Torch Logo™, AR Logo™

This book has been typeset in Wild Words and Serpentine Bold

Printed in China

British Library Cataloguing in Publication data:
a catalogue record for this book is available from the British Library

ISBN 978-1-4063-4066-2

www.walker.co.uk

...WE THEREFORE COMMIT HIS BODY TO THE *GROUND*, IN *SURE AND CERTAIN HOPE* OF THE RESURRECTION TO *ETERNAL LIFE*.

AMEN.

COME ON,

LET'S JUST GO *HOME*.

ALEX?

MY NAME IS *JOHN CRAWFORD*.

I'M WITH THE *ROYAL & GENERAL BANK*, AND I WANT YOU TO KNOW YOU HAVE ALL OUR CONDOLENCES.

IT'S AN ABSOLUTE *TRAGEDY*. A *CAR ACCIDENT!* IF ONLY HE'D BEEN WEARING A *SEAT BELT*...

THANK YOU—

THIS IS *ALAN BLUNT*, THE BANK *CHAIRMAN*.

HE'D LIKE A WORD.

ALEX?

WHIRRRRRR

SOUTH LONDON

WEIRD.

DOESN'T *LOOK* LIKE IT WAS IN A CRASH AT *ALL*...

THE *RIDER* CAR SHOULD HAVE BEEN DONE *TWO DAYS* AGO.

SO DO IT *NOW*, ALL RIGHT?

BUT I DIDN'T GET THE *PAPERWORK*...

JUST *DO* IT, HARRY. I'VE GOT TO GO TO *LIVERPOOL STREET*.

THE *STATION*?

WHERE *ELSE*, YOU BERK? I'M TAKING THEM THE *STUFF*...

WOW...

SKREEEEEEE

WHAT–?

?

BRAKKA BRAKKA BRAKKA BRAKKA

HEY—

EURGH!

I COULDN'T BELIEVE WHAT I WAS *DOING*. THIS GUY JUST CAME *AT ME*, AND...

WHAT WERE *THEY*... OW!

...DOING, JACK? AND WHY WERE THEY *HERE*?

COME *UPSTAIRS* AND SEE FOR *YOURSELF*...

CHELSEA

ALEX?

?

!!

HE'S ON HIS *WAY.*

FSSSH

AAAAAAAAAAAAAAAAAAA

KER—CHUNK!

GOOD MORNING, ALEX. SHOULDN'T YOU BE AT SCHOOL?

I ... WAS ... ON THE PLATFORM AT LIVERPOOL STREET... AND NOW I'M HERE...

THAT'S RIGHT.

SO WHAT IS THIS PLACE?

HOGWARTS?

HFF

HFF

KEEP THAT GUN ABOVE YOUR HEAD...

GBBL RGBR LRGR GLBR GR GL LBRGR!

BRECON BEACONS

YOU'RE NOT IN THE *PLAYGROUND* NOW, CUB! *MOVE IT!*

LET ME GIVE YOU A *HAND*, CUB.

NO, *WAI...T!*

AAAAAAAH

BLOOP!

HAHAHA!

HAHAHA HAHA!

HAHAHAHA!

KIYAAAI!

KRASH

THERE'S A *FIREPLACE*.

HOW DID *YOU* KNOW?

I SAW THE *CHIMNEY* ON THE WAY IN.

THE KID'S RIGHT. IT'S *CLEAR*.

YEAH, *RIGHT.* YOU THINK THEY'D JUST *LEAVE* IT IF THEY THOUGHT WE COULD ALL CLIMB *UP?*

YOU CAN'T. YOU'RE TOO BIG.

H.

HEY...!

HELP! SOMEBODY HELP!

?

WHERE *IS* EVERYONE?

OH, THEY
SLOPED OFF.

AAAAA AAAAA

SPLOSH!

CUTS, *BRUISES*, FRACTURED *LIMBS*...

IT'S A MIRACLE NO ONE WAS *KILLED!*

HE'S NOT A *CHILD*, HE'S A *LETHAL WEAPON.*

I'M *VERY* SORRY, MAJOR. WE WILL BE *TALKING* TO OUR MAN.

SORRY, *BOY.*

HE'S READY.

FINALLY,

THE MOST *GENEROUS* GIFT *EVER MADE* TO THE BRITISH NATION.

HEADLINES: EVERY SCH... THE UK TO BE GI... HE STORMBR...

THE *STORMBREAKER* HAS BEEN CALLED THE MOST *SOPHISTICATED* PERSONAL COMPUTER OF THE 21ST CENTURY...

...AND LAST MONTH, ITS MULTIBILLIONAIRE INVENTOR, *DARRIUS SAYLE*, MADE HIS ASTONISHING *ANNOUNCEMENT*.

LIVE

THAT'S *RIGHT*, VIVIEN. I WANT TO GIVE A *FREE* STORMBREAKER TO EVERY SCHOOL IN THE COUNTRY.

...PHISTICATED PC.

AND WHILE I'M *AT* IT, I WOULDN'T MIND GIVING *YOU* ONE TOO.

LIVE

REALLY, MR SAYLE!

PC. DARRIUS SAYLE S... ...ONTRIBU...

THE *PRIME MINISTER* HAS GIVEN HIS FULL SUPPORT...

THIS IS A *WONDERFUL* OPPORTUNITY FOR BRITISH SCHOOLS, AND I'M *HONOURED* THAT MR SAYLE HAS ASKED *ME* TO PRESS THE BUTTON THAT WILL BRING ALL THE COMPUTERS *ON-LINE*.

OOL IN THE UK TO BE GIVEN THE STORMBREAKER.

...JUST AS IT HAS *RECENTLY* COME TO LIGHT THAT HE AND MR SAYLE WERE AT *SCHOOL* TOGETHER.

FORTUNE

Inside
Darrius Sayle
....
....
....

WE DON'T **TRUST** HIM.

WHY NOT?

WELL, WE DON'T TRUST **ANYONE**. IT'S SORT OF WHAT WE'RE **FOR**.

KLIK

WE ALWAYS **THOUGHT** DARRIUS SAYLE WAS TOO **GOOD** TO BE **TRUE**. SO, SIX MONTHS AGO, WE SENT AN AGENT TO KEEP AN **EYE** ON HIM.

YOU MEAN MY **UNCLE**.

YES.

SAYLE HAS A **MANUFACTURING PLANT** IN **CORNWALL**, BUILT ON TOP OF WHAT USED TO BE A **TIN MINE**. IAN RIDER WENT THERE AS A **SECURITY GUARD**...

...AND HE **FOUND** SOMETHING. IN HIS LAST MESSAGE TO US, HE MENTIONED A **VIRUS**.

A **COMPUTER VIRUS**...?

WE DON'T KNOW. HE WAS ON HIS WAY TO **TELL** US, BUT HE NEVER ARRIVED.

SOMETHING'S GOING ON. WE NEED TO GET SOMEONE **IN** THERE TO TAKE A LOOK **AROUND**.

AND THIS MAY BE OUR **LAST CHANCE**.

DISK DRIVE WORLD

COMPETITION WINNER

Kevin Blake

WHY *ME?*

THIS IS *KEVIN BLAKE*, A COMPUTER NERD. SIX WEEKS AGO HE WON A *COMPETITION* IN THIS MAGAZINE.

EVER *READ* IT?

...

THE *FIRST PRIZE* WAS A *VISIT* TO CORNWALL AND A CHANCE TO TRY OUT THE *STORMBREAKER*.

HE'S DUE TO ARRIVE *TOMORROW*.

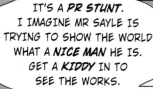

I'LL SHOW YOU.

IT'S A *PR STUNT.* I IMAGINE MR SAYLE IS TRYING TO SHOW THE WORLD WHAT A *NICE MAN* HE IS. GET A *KIDDY* IN TO SEE THE WORKS.

YOU'LL TAKE KEVIN'S PLACE.

BUT I'M NOTHING *LIKE* HIM.

DISK DRIVE WORLD

COMPETITION WINNER

Kevin Blake

WE'VE SPOKEN TO THE *EDITOR*.

!!

THERE'S JUST ONE *PROBLEM*...

I DON'T KNOW ANYTHING *ABOUT* COMPUTERS. I'M *NOT* A NERD.

BUT YOU SOON *WILL* BE.

WE ONLY HAVE *THREE DAYS* LEFT. THERE'S A LAUNCH AT THE *SCIENCE MUSEUM* NEXT FRIDAY. *70,000* STORMBREAKER COMPUTERS GOING LIVE...

...

WE *DON'T* WANT YOU TO GET INTO ANY *TROUBLE*, ALEX. JUST TAKE A LOOK *AROUND*. AND BE CAREFUL OF SAYLE. HE MAY *SEEM* CHARMING...

...BUT HE'S ABOUT AS CHARMING AS A *SNAKE*.

JUST KEEP YOUR *EYES* OPEN AND REPORT *BACK*.

BUT HOW WILL I DO *THAT*?

WE'LL SUPPLY YOU WITH A *TELECOMMUNICATIONS DEVICE*. THAT AND...

OTHER GADGETS.

I GET *GADGETS?*

EVENING NE[W]

SAYLE[
LAUNCHES T[
[S]TORMBREAK

IF YOU PAT HIS **HEAD**...

HIS **TAIL** WAGS.

HE ALSO OBEYS CERTAIN **VOICE** COMMANDS...

ROLL OVER!

KLUNK!

DELIGHTFUL, DON'T YOU THINK? WE ALSO HAVE ROBOT **CATS** AND **RODENTS—**

EXCUSE ME.

I'M LOOKING FOR SOMETHING TO TAKE TO **CORNWALL.**

GEEEE

GEEE

AH.

CORNWALL, YES.

COME WITH ME...

GEE GEEE

IT'S FROM **CORNWALL!**

GREETINGS FROM CORNWALL

BUT HE DIDN'T MEAN YOU TO GO THERE **NOW,** ALEX. THAT'S NOT WHAT HE **MEANT...**

IT'S ONLY A FEW DAYS, JACK.

I'LL BE **CAREFUL.**

YOU REALLY **PROMISE** ME?

I **PROMISE.**

AND ALEX...

WHAT?

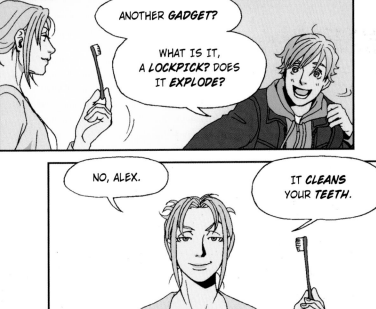

ANOTHER **GADGET?**

WHAT IS IT, A **LOCKPICK?** DOES IT **EXPLODE?**

NO, ALEX.

IT **CLEANS** YOUR **TEETH.**

MRS VOLE, IS THAT RIGHT? I'M THE EDITOR OF *DISC DRIVE WORLD*...

THEN THIS MUST BE *KEVIN*, JA?

KEVIN BLAKE!

THAT'S ME.

GUT. YOU SHOULD SAY *GOODBYE* NOW.

GOODBYE, KEVIN! I HOPE YOU FIND YOUR STAY VERY *INFORMATIVE!*

←ARRIVAL

CAR PARK→

I'M SURE IT *WILL* BE...

I AM *NADIA VOLE.* I WORK FOR *MR SAYLE* IN *PR.*

PUBLIC RELATIONS?

JA. THIS IS *PORT TALLON.* A *FISHING VILLAGE.*

PORT TALLON
Welcome
Careful Drivers

NICE PLACE.

NOT IF YOU ARE A *FISH.*

THE **MAN OF WAR** IS AN **OUTSIDER**.

IT'S **NINETY-NINE PER CENT WATER.** IT HAS NO **BRAINS,** AND NO **ANUS.**

IT'S **SILENT**, YET IT DEMANDS **RESPECT.** THOSE **TENTACLES** ARE COVERED IN **NEMATOCYSTS**... STINGING CELLS. IF YOU CAME INTO **CONTACT** WITH THEM, YOU'D DIE A VERY **MEMORABLE** DEATH.

...

I THINK I'M GOING TO **LIKE** YOU.

I'M TOO **YOUNG** TO DIE.

NO, NO, **NO.** I WOULDN'T BELIEVE **THAT.**

YOU'RE **NEVER** TOO YOUNG TO DIE.

WHAT THE...?

HIYA, CUDDLES.

MR SAYLE, THE **AMERICAN AMBASSADOR** IS ON LINE ONE.

FZZZZZ z z z z

IT SEEMS I'M **NOT** GOING TO BE ABLE TO **JOIN** YOU FOR LUNCH AFTER **ALL**, BUT I HOPE YOU'LL HAVE **DINNER** WITH ME TONIGHT.

IT'S BEEN QUITE A *WHILE* SINCE I FOUND MYSELF FACE TO FACE WITH A BRITISH *SCHOOL KID*... I CAN'T *WAIT* TO HEAR WHAT YOU THINK OF THE *STORMBREAKER*.

THIS IS MY PERSONAL ASSISTANT, *MR GRIN*.

HE SEEMS TO HAVE *CUT* HIMSELF *SHAVING*.

MR GRIN USED TO WORK IN A *CIRCUS*. IT WAS A NOVELTY *KNIFE-THROWING* ACT. FOR A *CLIMAX*, HE CAUGHT A *SPINNING KNIFE* BETWEEN HIS *TEETH*...

MURGH.

...UNTIL *ONE* NIGHT, HIS MOTHER *WAVED* TO HIM FROM THE FRONT ROW AND HE MADE A *MISTAKE* WITH HIS *TIMING*.

HE CAN'T *TALK*, BUT HE'LL SHOW YOU TO YOUR *ROOM* AND WE'LL MEET AGAIN *TONIGHT*. OK?

HAVE *FUN*.

BEEP

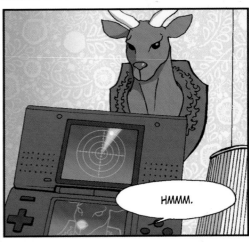

HMMM.

TIK!

YAAAAAA!

JA!
WHO *TAUGHT* YOU
ABOUT COMPUTERS,
KEVIN?

MY UNCLE.

HE IS A COMPUTER
WHIZ-KING?

YOU'RE USING *SLICE-MATRIX VIRTUAL REALITY* SOFTWARE, AREN'T YOU?

NO, HE WAS A *SECURITY GUARD*. BUT HE *DIED*.

HOW DID THAT *HAPPEN*?

I DON'T *KNOW*.

BUT *ONE* DAY I'LL FIND *OUT*.

PROGRAMMING COMPLETE

MAYBE.

BUT *NOT* TODAY.

YOU WILL START WITH *SCIENCE*. PRESS *ENTER* TO BEGIN.

SCIENCE, EH? GREAT...

...NOT.

UH-OH.

GOOD **MORNING**, MR SAYLE.

IS IT **READY** FOR ME?

YES, SIR. THIS WAY, PLEASE...

!

...THE **BACKUP SYSTEM**.

IT WILL SEND OUT A **SIGNAL** THAT WILL **INSTANTLY** ACTIVATE ALL **SEVENTY THOUSAND** COMPUTERS.

OF COURSE, IT SHOULDN'T BE **NEEDED**.

NO.

IT'S **EXCELLENT**. VERY...

...GOOD.

HMMM.

KEVIN?

DIESER **VERDAMMTE** JUNGE...

HMMM.

NICE **WEATHER** FOR THE TIME OF YEAR.

...BUT *ANYWAY.*

TELL ME, HOW DID YOU LIKE THE *STORMBREAKER?*

IT'S COOL.

"COOL." IS THAT *ALL* YOU CAN *SAY?*

YOU KNOW, KEVIN, IT STRIKES ME THAT YOU DON'T *TALK* VERY MUCH LIKE A COMPUTER *ENTHUSIAST.* NOR DO YOU *LOOK* LIKE ONE.

I'D HAVE SAID THE SAME ABOUT *YOU*, MR SAYLE.

GOOD *POINT*.

I'VE VERY MUCH *ENJOYED* MEETING YOU, KEVIN. I'M SURE YOU'LL HAVE A *LOT* TO TALK ABOUT WHEN YOU GET BACK TO *SCHOOL*.

SURE.

AND WHEN WE *LAUNCH* THE STORMBREAKERS TOMORROW...

I'LL BE THINKING *PARTICULARLY* OF YOU.

BRRRRING

CHELSEA

EXCUSE ME, FRÄULEIN.

I AM *LOOKING* FOR A PERSON CALLED *JACK*.

IS THIS ABOUT *ALEX*?

YES... YES, IT *IS*.

THEN YOU'D BETTER COME *IN*.

YOU ARE A *FRIEND* OF ALEX?

I *LOOK AFTER* HIM.

THIS IS ALEX, YES? AND THIS *MAN* WITH HIM ... HIS *FATHER*?

HIS *UNCLE*! LOOK, WHAT'S THIS *ABOUT*?

TELL ME...

WHO *IS* THIS BOY *ALEX RIDER*? WHAT IS HE *DOING*?

LET US **START.**

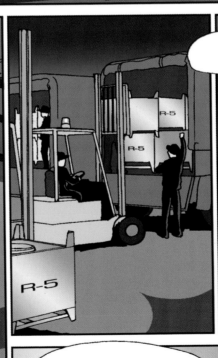

MR GREGOROVICH!

I'M GLAD YOU WERE ABLE TO **JOIN** US TONIGHT.

I DIDN'T **REALIZE** YOU WERE GOING TO COME **PERSONALLY.**

THIS IS THE **LAST BATCH.** MY PEOPLE WANTED TO BE **ASSURED** THAT THE OPERATION HAD ALL GONE ACCORDING TO **PLAN.**

MY PLAN. **MY** OPERATION.

WHY SHOULD **YOUR** PEOPLE THINK THAT ANYTHING MIGHT GO...

KRUMP

R-5

...WRONG?

R-5

IT IS **ALL RIGHT.** THE CONTAINER IS NOT COMPROMISED.

CARRY ON!

I'M SO SORRY.

I WON'T DO THAT AGAIN.

NO.

YOU WILL *NOT*.

BLAM!

MY PEOPLE DO NOT LIKE *MISTAKES*.

GET *BACK* TO *WORK*!

I TOLD YOU I **DIDN'T** WANT TO BE **INTERRUPTED–**

UNLESS IT WAS **IMPORTANT**.

AND **IS** IT?

WE JUST GOT **THIS** FROM ALEX RIDER.

"GREGOROVICH"? **YASSEN** GREGOROVICH?

IT **HAS** TO BE.

I THOUGHT HE WAS STILL IN **NORTH KOREA**.

IT SEEMS **NOT**.

THIS IS THE **PROOF** YOU NEED, ALAN. THE STORMBREAKER **LAUNCH** IS LESS THAN **24 HOURS** AWAY. **CANCEL** IT.

YES. YOU'RE **RIGHT**.

I'LL PUT A **CALL** INTO **DOWNING STREET**.

AND GET ALEX **OUT**.

HE'LL BE **FLYING** OUT AT TWELVE O'CLOCK TOMORROW **ANYWAY**. NO POINT MAKING SAYLE – OR **GREGOROVICH**, COME TO THAT – **SUSPICIOUS**.

YOU CAN **MEET** HIM IF YOU LIKE. TAKE HIM OUT FOR AN **ICE CREAM**.

WHAT?

HE'S DONE VERY **WELL**. HE DESERVES A **TREAT**.

ALEX *RIDER*...

I SUSPECTED HIM FROM THE *MOMENT* HE ARRIVED.

CORNWALL

AND HIS *UNCLE* WAS *IAN* RIDER... THE *SECURITY GUARD* WHO WAS ACTUALLY A *SPY!*

THESE *PEOPLE!* I MEAN, *REALLY*...!

WHAT DO YOU WANT ME TO *DO?*

GO TO HIS *ROOM.* WAKE HIM UP *GENTLY*... TRY NOT TO *ALARM* HIM.

THEN *KILL* HIM.

AND GET THAT *HAND* SEEN TO. I NEED YOU ON *TOP FORM* TODAY.

YES, MR SAYLE.

SNAP.

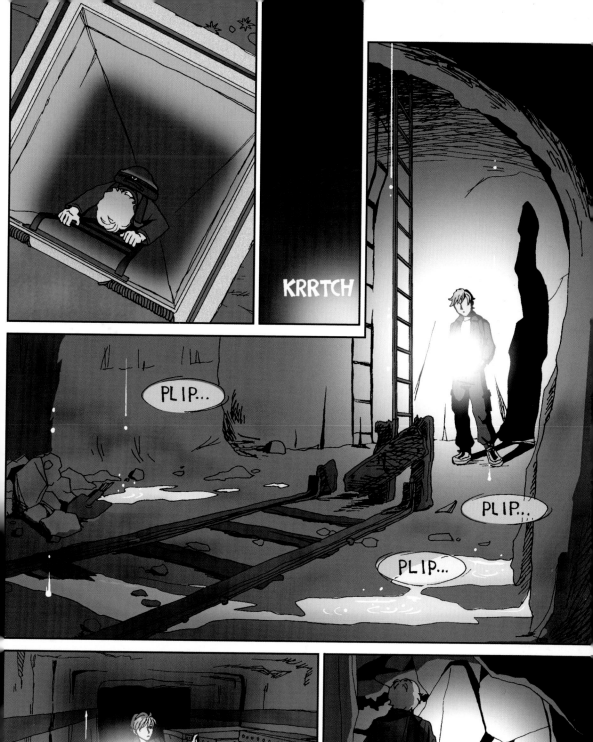

WHAT ARE YOU **DOING** HERE? WHO **ARE** YOU?

WHAT'S GOING **ON?** MY NAME'S **KEVIN BLAKE**... I WAS **INVITED** HERE.

IT IS A **GOOD ACT.** YOU DO IT VERY **WELL.** BUT YOU **SHOULDN'T** HAVE COME HERE.

WE CAN **TALK** ABOUT THIS...

I DO NOT **THINK** SO.

YES, WE **CAN!**

BE **CAREFUL!**

DO **NOT** DROP THAT...

"R5". WHAT IS IT?

PUT IT **BACK**, "KEVIN".

ALL RIGHT, THEN... WHAT'S THE WAY **OUT** OF HERE?

THANKS.

CATCH!

!

UP THERE.

BRAKKA BRAKKA SPTANG BRAKKA BRAKKA SPTANG

STOP! STOP!

YOU *IDIOT!* YOU MUST NOT FIRE *BULLETS* IN HERE!

OH!

OF COURSE, I'M *SORRY.* I WON'T DO THAT...

...AGAIN?

NO. YOU WILL *NOT.*

GOING SOMEWHERE, MEIN JUNGE?

YEAH.

I HAVE A *PLANE* TO CATCH.

NOT ANY *MORE*.

WHAT'S YOUR *NAME?*

YOU *KNOW* WHO I AM. I WON THE *COMPETITION.*

SIGH

MR GRIN?

THUNK

IF *THIS* IS HOW YOU TREAT THE *WINNER*, I'D *HATE* TO SEE WHAT HAPPENED TO THE *RUNNER-UP*.

YOU'RE *NOT* KEVIN BLAKE.

YOU'RE *ALEX RIDER*. YOUR *UNCLE* WAS PRETENDING TO BE A *SECURITY* GUARD, BUT *YASSEN GREGOROVICH* DEALT WITH *HIM*...

...AND *MI6* SENT *YOU* TO TAKE HIS PLACE.

SENDING A *FOURTEEN-YEAR-OLD* TO DO THEIR *DIRTY WORK*. NOT VERY *BRITISH*, I'D HAVE SAID. NOT *CRICKET*.

WHAT ARE YOU *DOING* HERE? WE *KNOW* YOU'RE PUTTING SOME KIND OF *VIRUS* INTO THE STORMBREAKER...

OH! IT'S... IT'S NOT A *COMPUTER* VIRUS, IS IT?

IT'S *THE REAL THING!*

VERY *CLEVER*, ALEX.

IT'S CALLED *R5*... A *GENETICALLY MODIFIED* VIRUS.

IT'S *VERY* NASTY.

BUT YOU'LL KILL **THOUSANDS** OF **PEOPLE!**

WHAT?

NO, NO, DON'T BE **SILLY.**

I'LL KILL **MILLIONS** OF THEM.

ALL BECAUSE YOU WERE **BULLIED** AT **SCHOOL?**

LOTS OF PEOPLE ARE BULLIED AT SCHOOL, BUT IT DOESN'T TURN **THEM** INTO **RAVING PSYCHOPATHS!**

TIME TO SAY **GOODBYE**, ALEX.

AS YOU MAY HAVE SEEN, I'M **PACKING UP** AND **LEAVING.** I'D **LOVE** TO STAY, BUT I HAVE A RATHER IMPORTANT APPOINTMENT IN **LONDON.**

SO I'LL LEAVE YOU TO **NADIA.**

THUNK

THAT WAS...

A GOOD **SHOT.**

EURGH.

ACTUALLY, IT WAS A **NEAR MISS.** YOU SHOULD WATCH YOUR **MOUTH.**

PLEEEH !

HAH

HAH

EW.

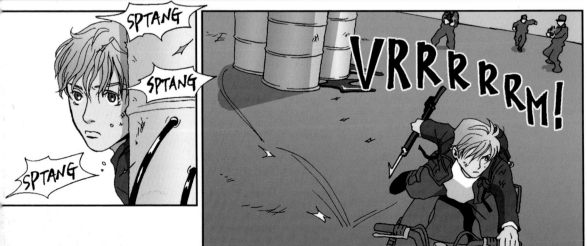

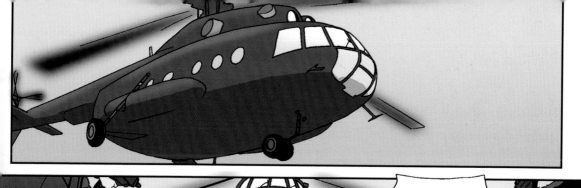

STOP HIM!

...FINAL DEPARTURE IS NOW. ALL PERSONNEL EVACUATE IMMEDIATELY.

REPEAT, FINAL DEPARTURE...

IMPRESSIVE.

HYDE PARK, LONDON

WE DON'T HAVE *TIME* FOR THIS NOW, MISS STARBRIGHT.

THE *PRIME MINISTER* IS...

WE DON'T KNOW.

WHAT DO YOU *MEAN*, YOU *DON'T KNOW?* YOU *PROMISED* ME YOU'D LOOK AFTER HIM!

CLAP

CLAP

CLAP

CLAP

LADIES AND GENTLEMEN, *THANK YOU.*

THE MESSAGE TODAY IS QUITE *CLEAR.*

"AND THAT MESSAGE IS *EDUCATION.* EDUCATION, EDUCATION,

AND..."

AND...

UM...

...AND *EDUCATION!*

AND *THAT* IS WHY I AM *DELIGHTED* TO ACCEPT THE *GENEROUS* OFFER MADE BY ONE OF OUR *FOREMOST ENTREPRENEURS*, AND *MY* OLD SCHOOL COLLEAGUE...

DARRIUS *SMELL.*

SAYLE!

DARRIUS *SAYLE!*

I WANT YOU TO KEEP FLYING *NORTH* UNTIL YOU RUN OUT OF *FUEL.* THEN YOU CAN *LAND,* OK?

NORGH.

BROOKLAND SCHOOL

YOU CAN LEAVE HIM TO **US**. DON'T **WORRY** ABOUT HIM.

YOU'VE DONE VERY **WELL**, ALEX. BUT YOU SHOULD **GO**, NOW.

WHAT ABOUT **SAYLE?**

...FINE.

HOW COULD THEY LET HIM SLIP **AWAY?**

IT'S NOT YOUR **PROBLEM**. I CAN'T BELIEVE I **EVER** LET YOU GET **MIXED UP** IN ALL THIS.

BUT IT'S **OVER** NOW, AND IT'S TIME YOU CAME **HOME**.

YEAH, BUT WHERE'S HE **GOING**...?

SOMEWHERE **REMOTE** AND **FAR AWAY** WHERE NOBODY WILL **EVER** FIND HIM. LIKE... PARAGUAY.

OR **IOWA**.

JACK! STOP THE **CAR!**

THAT'S IT!

SAYLE TOWER!

WHAT?

HE HAD A **MODEL** OF IT IN CORNWALL. HE WAS TALKING ABOUT A **BACKUP**, SOMETHING ABOUT A **MANUAL OVERRIDE**... THAT'S WHERE IT **IS**, AND THAT'S WHERE **HE** IS!

HE'S GOING TO SET OFF THE VIRUS **HIMSELF**!

COME **ON**, PUT YOUR **FOOT** DOWN!

I **CAN'T**!

WHY **NOT?** JACK, HE'LL KILL **EVERYONE**!

BECAUSE, ALEX, YOU'RE NOT IN **CORNWALL** ANY MORE.

WELCOME TO **LONDON TRAFFIC**.

NO...

ALEX?

ALEX, WHAT ARE YOU *DOING?*

I HAVE TO *STOP* HIM, JACK! I'LL *RUN* THERE IF—

ALEX?

WHAT ARE *YOU* DOING HERE?

SABINA...?

I THOUGHT YOU HAD *MUMPS.*

I GOT *BETTER.*

LOOK, SABINA, I NEED YOUR *HELP.* I HAVE TO BE ON THE *OTHER* SIDE OF *LONDON,* RIGHT *NOW!*

WHY?

I...

HAVE TO *SAVE* THE *WORLD?*

OH,

OK.

THAT'S RIGHT, **MRS JONES!**

I DON'T **KNOW** WHAT HER **FIRST NAME** IS! I'M NOT SENDING HER A **BIRTHDAY** CARD, THIS IS **URGENT!** STOP MAKING ME...

...JUMP OVER HURDLES...

YAAAH!

ALEX...

KEEP GOING!

AAAAH!

WOOOAH!

WHAT THE-?

DAMNED *LUNATICS!*

AFTER THEM!

OH, NO...
DON'T LOOK ROUND!

WHY NOT?

TRUST ME!

SKREECH!

AAAH!

WHOOPS!

SORRY!

THANKS, SABINA!

WAIT...!

STOP RIGHT THERE!

NOT *AGAIN*...

WHUD!

!

SCHOOLBOY TRICK.

OODOWOOARRRRrrr

ALEX, WAIT FOR *ME!*

UHHH... STOP...

OH, *SHUSH.*

OOOOUUUUH...

MEN.

BING!

COME ON...

COME ON...

BOOT COMPLETED

INITIATING TRANSMITTER ALIGNMENT

WHAT...?

KLIK!

KLIK!

KLIK!

NO!

RIDER.

PUT IT **BACK**.

I SAID *PUT IT BACK.*

NOW.

SKREEECH!!

TAKE UP *POSITIONS!*

DON'T YOU *DARE* HURT THEM!

HEH.

HEH HEH HEH.

WHUMP

TWANG

ALEX, I'M SLIPPING...!

ALL RIGHT...

I'LL *SWING* YOU ONTO THE *BALCONY!*

NO, *DON'T!*

THE CABLE WILL *BREAK!*

I CAN DO IT!

DO YOU *TRUST* ME?

NO!

TYPICAL.

!

HOLD ON...

AAAAAAH!

UNH!

TWANG

TWANG

PING

SAYLE HAD BECOME AN *EMBARRASSMENT* TO THE PEOPLE I *WORK* FOR.

WHAT ABOUT *ME*?

I HAVE NO *INSTRUCTIONS* CONCERNING YOU.

THIS DOESN'T *CHANGE* ANYTHING.

YOU *KILLED* MY *UNCLE*. YOU'RE STILL MY *ENEMY*.

I HAVE *MANY* ENEMIES.

THIS *ISN'T OVER*, GREGOROVICH!

I THINK IT *IS*, ALEX. GO BACK TO *SCHOOL*.

YOU DO NOT *BELONG* TO MY WORLD, AND YOU SHOULD *FORGET* ABOUT ME.

I'LL *NEVER* FORGET YOU.

THAT IS *YOUR* CHOICE.

YOU DON'T **HAVE** TO WALK WITH ME TO **SCHOOL**.

I **JUST** WANT TO MAKE SURE YOU **GET** THERE, YOU KNOW?

BROOKLAND SCHOOL

HI, ALEX! YOUR **MUMPS** CLEARED UP, THEN?

HI!

WHAT DOES **HE** TEACH? AND HOW COME YOU NEVER MENTIONED HIM TO **ME** BEFORE...?

THE END?

ANTHONY HOROWITZ (BA/Nielsen Author of the Year) is one of the most popular children's writers working today. His hugely successful Alex Rider series has sold over ten million copies worldwide and won numerous awards, including the Children's Book of the Year Award for ARK ANGEL at the British Book Awards and the Red House Children's Book Award for SKELETON KEY. He scripted the blockbuster movie STORMBREAKER from his own novel, and also writes extensively for TV, with programmes including MIDSOMER MURDERS, COLLISION, INJUSTICE and FOYLE'S WAR. Anthony Horowitz is the author of THE HOUSE OF SILK: THE NEW SHERLOCK HOLMES NOVEL. He is married to television producer Jill Green and lives in Clerkenwell with his two sons, Nicholas and Cassian, and the ghost of their dog, Lucky.

www.anthonyhorowitz.com

ANTONY JOHNSTON, who wrote the script for this book, is a veteran author of comics and graphic novels, from superheroes such as DAREDEVIL and WOLVERINE, to science-fiction adventures like WASTELAND and DEAD SPACE, and even thrillers such as THE COLDEST CITY and JULIUS. He also writes videogames, including many of the DEAD SPACE series, and other games like BINARY DOMAIN and XCOM. His debut fiction novel FRIGHTENING CURVES won an IPPY award for Best Horror. Antony lives in North-West England with his partner Marcia, his dogs Connor and Rosie, and far too many gadgets with apples printed on them.

www.antonyjohnston.com

The artwork in this graphic novel is the work of two artists, **KANAKO DAMERUM** and **YUZURU TAKASAKI,** who collaborate on every illustration. Although living on opposite sides of the globe, these Japanese sisters work seamlessly together via the Internet.

Living and working in Tokyo, **YUZURU** produced all the line work for these illustrations using traditional means. The quality of her draughtsmanship comes from years of honing her skills in the highly competitive world of manga.

KANAKO lives and works out of her studio in London. She managed and directed the project as well as colouring and rendering the artwork digitally using her wealth of knowledge in graphic design.

www.manga-media.com
www.thorogood.net

Collect all the Alex Rider books

ALEX RIDER MISSION 1 : STORMBREAKER
ANTHONY HOROWITZ

ALEX RIDER MISSION 2 : POINT BLANC
ANTHONY HOROWITZ

ALEX RIDER MISSION 3 : SKELETON KEY
ANTHONY HOROWITZ

ALEX RIDER MISSION 4 : EAGLE STRIKE
ANTHONY HOROWITZ

ALEX RIDER MISSION 5 : SCORPIA
ANTHONY HOROWITZ

ALEX RIDER MISSION 6 : ARK ANGEL
ANTHONY HOROWITZ

ALEX RIDER MISSION 7 : SNAKEHEAD
ANTHONY HOROWITZ

ALEX RIDER MISSION 8 : CROCODILE TEARS
ANTHONY HOROWITZ

ALEX RIDER MISSION 9 : SCORPIA RISING
ANTHONY HOROWITZ

and the graphic novels

ALEX RIDER
ANTHONY HOROWITZ
ANTONY JOHNSTON
KANAKO AND YUZURU
THE GRAPHIC NOVEL
POINT BLANC

ALEX RIDER
ANTHONY HOROWITZ
ANTONY JOHNSTON
KANAKO AND YUZURU
THE GRAPHIC NOVEL
SKELETON KEY

ALEX RIDER
ANTHONY HOROWITZ
ANTONY JOHNSTON
KANAKO AND YUZURU
THE GRAPHIC NOVEL
EAGLE STRIKE

alexrider.com